Beyond Imagination

Pacific Press®
Publishing Association

Nampa, Idaho | Oshawa, Ontario, Canada
www.pacificpress.com

Is there more to life than we know?

BEYOND IMAGINATION

BALDWIN • GIBSON • THOMAS

Design by Steve Lanto
Cover design resources from iStockphoto.com

Copyright © 2013 by Pacific Press® Publishing Association
Printed in the United States of America
All rights reserved

You can obtain additional copies of this book by calling toll-free
1-800-765-6955 or by visiting http://www.adventistbookcenter.com.

ISBN 13: 978-0-8163-4514-4
ISBN 10: 0-8163-4514-7

13 14 15 16 17 • 5 4 3 2 1

Contents

Beyond
Imagination

Stand outside on a clear night and look up. How far can you see? How much can you see? Have you ever seen the Milky Way? On very special dark nights, if you live far enough from city lights, you can see a broad swatch of lights across the heavens. It's a view in toward the center of our Milky Way galaxy, where the stars seem so close together that they blend into a milky white glow.

Since our solar system rotates around a pale star in one of our galaxy's spiral arms, we are a long way from the center of the action. We're in the suburbs of our own galaxy, a tiny spot in a sea of roughly two hundred billion stars.

Two hundred billion stars—but even on the darkest night with the clearest skies, our human eyes can only actually see about three thousand of them at any given moment. There are less than nine thousand stars visible from earth with the naked eye, and those are "nearby" in our own Milky Way.

We used to think that the earth was the center of the universe, that the sun and all the stars rotated around it. But as soon as the telescope

The Milky Way galaxy

was invented, we discovered that we were wrong. Each time we've invented a stronger telescope, we've learned that the universe is bigger than we thought. We've discovered a universe so big that not just our little planet, or our weak sun, but our entire Milky Way galaxy is just a spot, a blip, barely worth noticing.

How big is the universe?

How big is the universe? Bigger than we think. Bigger than we can even imagine! Let's see if we can wrap our minds around some of the numbers.

How far have you traveled in the last year? Twenty thousand miles? Fifty thousand? Many people who fly for business regularly travel one hundred thousand or more miles every year. We can easily see the moon when we look up into the sky—it's only about two hundred fifty thousand miles away. We can also see the sun—although we shouldn't look directly at it. It looks as if it is about the same size as the moon, but really it's just a lot farther away—ninety-three million miles. It's so far away that it takes sunlight over eight minutes to reach the earth!

If the earth were the size of a coin, the sun would be as big as a nine-foot beach ball.

How big is the sun? About a million earths would fit inside it. If the earth were the size of a coin, the sun would be as big as a nine-foot beach ball. That is almost too big to imagine! The sun has to be the biggest thing in the universe, doesn't it?

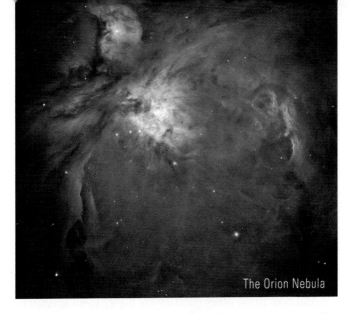
The Orion Nebula

Well, no. Have you ever looked up to see the constellation Orion the Hunter in the sky? Betelgeuse, the bright star on Orion's top-left shoulder, is so big that if it was the star in our solar system instead of the sun, it wouldn't fit into the big circle the earth makes when it circles the sun from ninety-three million miles away. It wouldn't even fit inside the orbit of Jupiter—and that's 484 million miles from the sun!

But the largest known star is called Canis Majoris. It's so big that if earth was the size of a coin and if our sun was a nine-foot beach ball, Canis Majoris would be about two and a half miles wide!

And if the earth was the size of a coin and the sun as large as a nine-foot ball, how far away would the sun be? About the length of a football field. In fact, if our entire solar system—the sun and all the planets—was the size of a coin, the sun would be visible only under a microscope, and the nearest star would be three hundred feet away. If you could travel at the speed of light—that's 186,000 miles per second—it would still take one hundred thousand years just to travel across our galaxy!

If our whole galaxy was the size of a coin—remember, that's two hundred billion stars—our solar system would be too small to be seen under a regular microscope. The other galaxies out there would still be from one foot to one thousand feet away.

So many galaxies! So many stars!

And how many other galaxies are there? In an attempt to see deeper in space than ever before, astronomers focused

The Whirlpool galaxy

the Hubble telescope on a seemingly empty patch of the night sky. Empty—no visible stars, galaxies, or anything. They focused on nothing for eleven days, then carefully examined the photograph. In this tiny little spot—about 3 percent of the size of a full moon—they found more than ten thousand galaxies—not stars, but entire galaxies of stars—each with billions of stars.

When they focused the Hubble telescope there for twenty-three days, they found that they could see even more galaxies—almost twice as many. Based on these deep field studies, astronomers estimate that there at least 175 billion galaxies within their current view from earth. How many stars would that be? If we consider our galaxy's two hundred billion to be average, there are something like 350,000,000,000,000,000,000,000 stars by my calculation. Until we develop the technology to see deeper or farther into space, anyway.[1]

Hubble telescope

Hubble ultra deep field

Think about it this way: the next time you're on the beach, pick up a handful of sand. If the estimates are right, there are more stars in the universe than there are grains of sand on all the beaches in the world. What we see when we look up—it's only a handful of sand.

We've certainly learned that earth is not the center of the universe. But for many years we've wondered whether or not earth was unique—whether it was the only planet in the whole universe. Recently, we've learned that most star systems have planets. In our galaxy alone, the estimate is that there are more than a billion planets.[2]

How many of those planets have animals or plants of some kind? We don't know the answer to that question yet. And could there be intelligent life on some other planet? That's the big question all astronomers are asking.

The wonders of the universe are beyond imagination! And we haven't even mentioned nebulas, quasars, black holes, or any of the many other fascinating objects in our universe. Can it really all have come into existence accidentally?

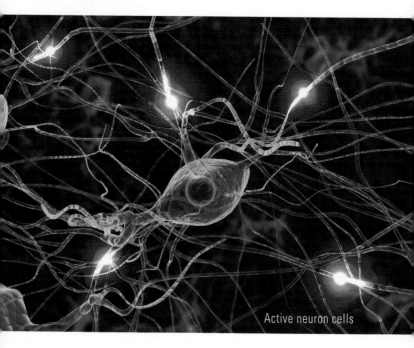

Active neuron cells

Journey of discovery

And it's a bigger question than just the universe—what about the astounding wonders of life around us here on earth? And the wonders of our own human bodies? There are more neuron cells in your brain than there are stars in our galaxy!

In this book, we will explore the wonders of not only life around us but also the wonder of our own existence. Some people believe that science offers all the answers we seek. But many find that scientific searches leave an empty space in their hearts.

Since the earliest days of human history, people have struggled with the big questions of life. Why are we here? Where are we going? What happens to us when we die? Why is there so much evil and suffering in the world?

Science isn't asking these questions. It doesn't offer answers for some of the deepest longings of the human heart. But that doesn't mean that those answers can't be found.

Come along on a journey of discovery, a journey to seek out the wonders around us, to learn what ties those amazing things together. Come and discover not only life that we may have never imagined, but even more remarkable, a love that is beyond imagination.

1. http://blogs.discovermagazine.com/crux/2012/10/10/how-many-galaxies-are-there-in-the-universe-the-redder-we-look-the-more-we-see/.
2. http://www.jpl.nasa.gov/news/news.php?release=2013-002.

The Day
the Universe
Changed Forever

In 1609, a man named Galileo Galilei was living in Italy, in a university town called Padua, when news came that inventors in the Netherlands had created a device that made objects appear closer than they were. Galileo was skeptical that such a thing was possible, but soon learned how the device worked, and made a better one of his own. Galileo's spyglass made things seem nine times closer and could be used for military and commercial purposes. Galileo continued tinkering with his invention and before long he had a twenty-power telescope. Around the first of December of that year, Galileo pointed his telescope at the moon. What he saw forever changed our understanding of the universe around us.

In those days, most people thought that the moon was perfectly round and smooth. The ancient philosopher Aristotle had taught that the heavens were perfect and the earth was imperfect. To his surprise, Galileo saw that the surface of the moon was rough, with mountains and plains. The "imperfect" moon surface led Galileo to rethink everything he thought he

The moon over the earth

The "imperfect" moon

knew about the universe. The heavens, he decided, must be as "imperfect" as the earth.

While Galileo was studying the moon, he was surprised to discover something else. He noticed that the sky around the moon was filled with stars—stars no one had ever seen before. The "Milky Way" was well known, but it was thought to be a cloud of gas or dust particles. Of course, the Milky Way is really a large number of stars that are too faint and close together for the eye to see clearly. For the first time, Galileo could see that there were far more than just the 1,022 stars that the ancient Greeks had counted. This discovery helped scientists realize that the universe is enormously large.

> The Milky Way is really a large number of stars that are too faint and close together for the eye to see clearly.

A few weeks later, Galileo was surprised again. While looking at the planet Jupiter through his telescope, Galileo discovered small "stars" that seemed to stay close to Jupiter. Surprisingly, these "stars" first appeared on one side of Jupiter, then disappeared, and then reappeared on the other side of Jupiter. Later, they disappeared again and reappeared on the first side. Galileo realized that they were orbiting Jupiter like our moon orbits the earth. Galileo saw three of them at first, then a fourth. Today, we can see a total of eleven moons circling Jupiter.

Jupiter and an orbiting moon

This discovery that moons circled something else besides earth supported an idea that astronomer Nicolaus Copernicus was suggesting: the earth is not the center of the universe. A scientific revolution was underway, a revolution that still affects us today.

A new picture of the universe

Our picture of the universe has changed dramatically since that fateful night in 1609. We now realize that far from being the center of the universe, we're only a part of an unimpressive solar system located in a side branch of one of many galaxies. We can see that the same laws of nature that operate on earth also operate in the solar system and beyond. We have discovered that the universe is unimaginably large, with many different kinds of stars and many other objects, some of which we know very little about and have barely even begun to understand.

We can see that the universe contains enormous amounts of matter and energy. In spite of imperfect craters in the moon and on other planets, the universe is organized into very specific structures—solar systems, galaxies, and clusters of galaxies. And we have discovered certain evidence that the universe is not eternal, that it had a beginning.

Today, we are used to the idea that new discoveries may change our ideas—new technology, new medicines, new ways of thinking. But in Galileo's time, this was not so easily accepted. When Galileo turned his telescope toward the moon on that December night in 1609, he could not have imagined how much his discoveries would change our way of thinking.

An unimaginably large universe

As we have seen, the universe is much larger than Galileo realized. Our earth is part of a system of eight planets and many smaller objects that revolve around the sun. Our sun is one of billions of stars in the universe, and is far distant from any other star. The closest star to us, Proxima Centauri, is about twenty-five trillion miles, or about 4.2 light-years away. In space, the distances are so large that we don't use miles or kilometers to measure them. We use light-years, the distance light travels in a year going 186,000 miles per second. Remember, it takes eight minutes for light to reach us from the sun, ninety-three million miles away.

If we tried to travel to Proxima Centauri in a rocket going sixteen thousand miles per hour, we would never make it. It would take 175,000 years to travel that far!

Our sun

Think of it this way: if you made a map to show the distance from our earth to Proxima Centauri, and used the period at the end of this sentence to represent the size of the earth, Proxima Centauri would be about one hundred miles away. And this is the closest star! Most stars are much farther away than this, and all of them would take impossibly long times to reach by any technology available to us. The universe is enormously larger than Galileo or anyone before him had ever imagined.

A universe of energy

The universe contains an unimaginable amount of matter and energy. We think of the universe as being made of stars, but it also contains many things we cannot see. As we saw earlier, we do not know exactly how many stars there are in the universe. But if the two hundred billion stars in our Milky Way galaxy are on the average, and there are at least 175 billion galaxies, then there must be at least 350 billion trillion stars.

And the visible stars may form only about one-tenth of the mass of the universe. The rest is in the form of "dark

The Antennae Galaxies

matter," which includes objects too small or too faint for us to detect. It also includes "black holes," which are so massive that even light cannot escape their gravitational field. All this matter contains an enormous amount of energy.

The Sombrero galaxy

The energy of the universe is also beyond our ability to comprehend. Each star shines brightly because it produces so much heat that the atoms glow. Our own star—the sun—has a temperature of more than fifteen million degrees (Kelvin). This huge amount of energy is enough to provide heat to warm our planet and light, which allows plants to grow and produce our food. And remember, our sun is not a large or hot star compared to most others. The amount of energy in the universe is beyond our ability to measure or even imagine.

The size of the universe and the vast energy it contains naturally lead us to one question: Where did it come from?

A beginning for the universe

Imagine you hold a balloon in your hands. Now take a pen and mark spots on the balloon one inch apart. When you hold the balloon to your lips and fill it with air, what happens to the distance between the spots? As the material of the balloon between the spots expands, all the spots move farther apart from each other. Scientists have discovered that something similar is happening to the stars. They are all moving apart from each other. Apparently, the universe is expanding, like a balloon expands with air.

> Matter is not scattered around randomly in the universe, but is mostly clumped into stars, planets, and other objects.

If the universe is expanding, it must have been smaller in the past. The farther we look into the past, the smaller the universe would be. If we look back far enough, the universe would have shrunken down too small to see, then to an invisible point. This would be the beginning of the universe. From that invisible point, the entire universe has grown to its present size. Based on this reasoning, scientists began to believe that the universe had a beginning.

Modern scientists were divided at first over whether to accept the idea. One astronomer, Sir Fred Hoyle, was so opposed to this idea that he mockingly referred to it as the "big bang." The name caught on, and we still refer to the theory as the big bang theory. Further studies and discoveries seemed to support the big bang theory, and most scientists now accept it.

The big bang theory raises some very big questions. What would cause the universe to appear from a tiny point, or from nothing? Could this happen accidently? Or is there something or someone behind the creation of the universe?

A designed universe

We can get some clues about the origin of the universe by studying what it is like today. The orderly structure and precise properties of the universe, for instance, are important clues to its origin. Matter is not scattered around randomly in the universe, but is mostly clumped into stars, planets, and other objects. Stars are not scattered randomly either, but are clumped into galaxies. And galaxies are often clumped into galactic clusters and superclusters.

Most amazing of all, the universe has exactly the kinds of properties needed for life to exist. How do we explain this kind of order in the universe? There seem to be three possible answers: natural law, chance, and intelligent design. Let's look at each of these as potential causes for the order in the universe.

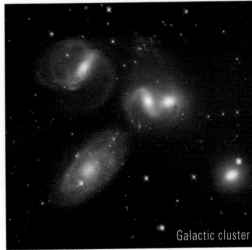
Galactic cluster

Natural law

Is it natural for the universe to have such a specific structure? No. There is no law that says the universe must be arranged so that it will form into planets, stars, galaxies

Butterfly Nebula.

and clusters. It could as easily be made up of just clouds of dust. Scientifically, the second law of thermodynamics tells us that order breaks down over time. That means the universe was more orderly in the past than it is now. Tracing this idea back to the beginning of the universe means that the universe must have been created with extremely precise original conditions.

So the order of the universe cannot be the result of some natural law that requires it. That leaves the question of whether the order in the universe is just the result of some lucky chance, or the product of an intelligent creator.

Chance

If life is going to exist, then the properties of the universe have to be very precise—very specific. For example, if the universe expanded too rapidly, matter would spread apart too quickly to form galaxies, and there would be no planets. On the other hand, if the universe expanded too slowly, matter would all clump into one giant lump, and there would still be no planets. Either way, life would not be possible.

The expansion rate of the universe must be so precisely fixed that a difference of one part in 10^{55} (the number 10 followed by 54 zeros) would throw it off. The chances of that happening are less than the chances of winning the lottery five times in a row. Think about that. If someone did win the lottery five times in a row, would you believe that it happened by chance? Neither would anyone else! Clearly, chance is not a good explanation for the precise conditions in the big bang.

Intelligent design

More than anything else, it's the orderly structure of the universe that suggests that the universe was intelligently and purposefully planned. But scientists have determined that the universe has many finely tuned properties—exactly the ones required in order for life to exist. For example, life requires molecules to construct bodies, carry

Dust clouds in the Eagle Nebula

BEYOND IMAGINATION

energy, and provide nutrients. But molecules could not exist unless there was an extremely precise balance among the masses of the various atomic particles and the forces holding them together. Many scientists have commented on the precisely tuned features of our universe, and suggested that they appear to be the result of intelligent planning.

Neither natural law nor chance provides a satisfactory explanation for the exquisite design of the universe. The best explanation—the one that fits what we see in our universe—is that it was intentionally created by One with unlimited power and intelligence.

Conclusion

Our picture of the universe has changed dramatically since the time of Galileo. We now realize the universe is vastly larger and more complex than anyone could have imagined only a few hundred years ago. Until recently, many scientists thought the universe had always existed and would always exist without ever changing in any way. Now we know it had a beginning, and is highly ordered and finely tuned for the survival of life. Even though our understanding of the universe is always changing, one thing remains the same. Humans have always been fascinated by what is "out there." And it has led them to ask big questions about our own existence.

We'll keep exploring this idea as we focus a little closer to home—our own world and some of the marvels of the living creatures around us.

The Design
of the Earth

Chapter 3

There are few places in the world with more varieties of fascinating life than Australia's Great Barrier Reef. This enormous complex of reefs runs along the northeastern coast of the Land Down Under. Snorkeling there, you can see giant clams with their exposed mantles green with microscopic algae. Schools of colorful fish appear and disappear among the coral. The coral itself is a wonder to behold, a living organism miles long in a rainbow of colors and an endless array of shapes and sizes. Hidden in its depths are colonies of wonderful life-forms and amazing creatures.

Amazing creatures

What may be even more wondrous are some of the hidden details in the lives of these creatures. The giant clam, for example, has an interesting, mutually beneficial relationship with the tiny, one-celled alga called Symbiodinium. The clam—which really is giant-sized at four feet long and up to five hundred pounds—sits on the ocean floor with its two shells spread apart and its fleshy mantle exposed to sunlight. The algal

A clown fish on Australia's Great Barrier Reef

cells live within the cells of the clam's mantle, where they produce food by photosynthesis. A single clam may have millions or even billions of algal cells in its tissues. The algae obtain nutrients from the clam, and the clam gets part of its nutrients from food produced by the algae. This is a kind of cooperative relationship in which each partner benefits the other. Together, the giant clam and its algae can live for up to one hundred years.

Cooperative relationships are common among living organisms. Some, like the giant clam and the tiny alga, are very specific. In the big picture, all living organisms interact in ways that are mutually beneficial. Plants capture energy from sunlight and use it to convert water and carbon dioxide into food. Oxygen is released in the process.

Animals recombine the oxygen and food to release the energy for growth and movement. Carbon dioxide is produced in this process, which is used by the plants to produce food. The cycle continues, and the mutually beneficial interactions among plants and animals make survival possible for a rich diversity of living creatures, including humans.

The palolo worm is another interesting creature that lives in the corals of the Great Barrier Reef, and in many other places in the South Pacific. These worms, which look a little like a flattened earthworm, grow to about a foot in length, and live in tunnels in blocks of coral, where they feed on algae. The palolo worm is best known in Samoa, where it is an important part of the local culture. Each year, at a certain time, the Samoans wade out into the sea to collect the eggs of the palolo worm. This event is so predictable and so significant to the local people that it is used to help set the local calendar.

> In the big picture, all living organisms interact in ways that are mutually beneficial.

Scientists have discovered some remarkable facts about these Samoan worms. At the season for breeding, the palolo worms grow a tail that fills with eggs or sperm. During spawning, the tail breaks off and carries the eggs to the surface, where they are fertilized. Nearly all the worms in an area release their eggs together. The precise timing of this behavior is especially impressive. Spawning

3—B.I.

begins just seven days after a full moon that occurs between October 8 and November 23. It may be repeated for

Shearwater

two or sometimes three days. The peak of swarming is a period of about thirty minutes at high tide, just after midnight. Somehow, the worms can sense when the time is right, and they all produce their eggs at about the same time. So many eggs are produced that the Samoans are able to collect them for food.

Worms living in other regions may spawn in a different month, but spawning is always rather precisely timed and coordinated. Somehow, these worms are able to coordinate their spawning. Because they all respond to the same signal in their environment, their species survives.

A crow-sized bird known as the Shearwater is another creature that might be spotted along the Great Barrier Reef at certain times of the year. Shearwaters spend their entire life at sea, except for when they are breeding. When breeding, they nest in burrows which they dig for themselves.

Shearwaters are marvelous navigators. They wander freely over the oceans without losing their way. They leave their nesting burrows before dawn and return to them after dark, which means they must be able to find the exact location not just of their island, but their burrow on the island—in the dark. Scientists are not sure exactly how they can do that!

During the day, Shearwaters fly over the ocean, feeding on small fish and squid near the surface of the ocean. The amazing ability of these birds to navigate was tested by an experiment in Great Britain using the Manx Shearwater.

Many other creatures have the ability to travel for hundreds or even thousands of miles and return to the exact starting place.

Scientists flew a group of Manx Shearwaters from Great Britain to Boston, in the United States, and a second group to Venice, Italy. Both groups of birds returned to their nesting burrows in Great Britain within about two weeks. Shearwaters do not normally fly over land at all, so it was even more remarkable that they could find their way home.

Sea turtle

Another species, the Sooty Shearwater, migrates from the Antarctic waters to California, Alaska, and Japan, and returns, a trip of thirty-nine thousand miles. Shearwaters are truly one of the wonders among living creatures.

Many other creatures have the ability to travel for hundreds or even thousands of miles and return to the exact starting place. Pacific salmon are famous for their ability to return to the place where they grew up. Sea turtles may travel thousands of miles between the Caribbean and islands in the Atlantic Ocean. Millions of songbirds migrate annually between North and South America or between Europe and Africa. Their migratory instinct and the ability to keep track of their location over such long distances are among the most unimaginable marvels of living creatures.

Our amazing world

Besides these marvelous creatures, there are many other examples of amazing life that could be explored—the production of light by the firefly, the generation of electricity by the electric catfish, the ability of the bat to navigate in the dark using echolocation, the transformation of a caterpillar into a beautiful butterfly, and many more.

But we don't often consider the kind of world that is needed in order for life to thrive.

As scientists have explored our universe, they have become more and more aware of how unique and well-designed

Monarch butterfly

our world is. They see more and more what exact and special conditions are needed if life is going to survive. The earth itself appears to be carefully designed for life.

Living organisms must have exactly the right combination of environmental conditions. This includes a suitable source of energy (such as sunlight), raw materials for constructing cells and tissues (nutrients), a suitable medium in which the chemistry of life can occur (water), and a suitable temperature for the necessary chemical reactions. As far as we know, no other place in the universe has the right combination of these features to support living organisms (although some possibilities have recently been discovered—which should be very interesting!).

As we all know, sunlight provides the energy for living organisms. A few bacteria get their energy from chemical reactions deep in the sea, but these are the exception. Sunlight is such a common, ordinary feature of our daily lives that it's easy to forget how special it is.

Light is a form of energy known as electromagnetic radiation. The strength of this kind of energy varies greatly.

Some types, such as gamma rays, are so powerful they easily destroy life. Other types, such as radio waves, are so weak they could not provide the energy needed for life. Visible light, the light we can see, has a moderate amount of energy. It is strong enough to trigger some chemical reactions, but not strong enough to tear apart the molecules that make up the bodies of living organisms. The fact that our sun produces this kind of light is one of the most important reasons why life can survive here. Most stars in our universe don't provide the right amount of energy to support life as we know it. Our world and our sun are special!

> The sun not only produces light to provide the energy living things need, it also produces the right amount of heat for life on earth.

The sun not only produces light to provide the energy living things need, it also produces the right amount of heat for life on earth. The temperature of the earth is determined by the heat output from the sun, the distance from the sun to the earth, and the ability of the earth to hold on to the heat. If the earth was farther from the sun, it would be too cold. If closer to the sun, it would be too hot. Carbon dioxide and water vapor in our atmosphere help hold the heat from the sun and maintain a suitable temperature. If our atmosphere had too much of these gases, our world would be too hot. If our atmosphere did not have any of these gases, our world would be too cold. Our favorable temperature is also maintained by the speed the earth rotates on its axis, and by the way the continents and oceans are distributed across the surface of the earth.

The survival of life on our planet depends on the right interaction between the earth, its atmosphere, the output of the sun, and the distance between the earth and the sun. If one of these factors were to change dramatically, life on our world could easily become extinct.

Life also requires a source of raw materials and a way for them to react chemically. The earth provides these in the right combinations. Water is one of the most important raw materials for life, and our earth has a lot of water. Some of the other planets and moons in our solar system appear to have some water, but not stable bodies of liquid water like our earth has. Water is so crucial for life that scientists looking for life on other planets look first for water. If there is no water, there's not much reason to look for life.

> The survival of life on our planet depends on the right interaction between the earth, its atmosphere, the output of the sun, and the distance between the earth and the sun.

Water is important for life. It provides a medium in which chemical reactions can occur. It dissolves many substances and transports them in the environment, and also throughout the bodies of living organisms. Without water, many chemical reactions necessary for life could not happen.

Water also moves heat throughout the environment, helping maintain a moderate temperature over the earth. Large bodies of water help moderate the climate, so that coastal areas usually have a milder climate than areas farther from the sea. Water also helps living organisms maintain a favorable temperature. It helps remove heat from our own bodies when it evaporates from our skin. If our world did not have so much water, it would have less life.

Water has many other properties that help life survive. The fact that ice floats enables fish to survive in lakes even when the surface freezes. If ice sank, the lake would eventually freeze up from bottom to top and kill most of the creatures in the lake. Water absorbs oxygen, needed by fish and other aquatic organisms. Water molecules tend to cling together, which is an important factor enabling water to move upward to the tops of tall trees. Liquid water flows easily, which permits it to move freely along the surface or through the soil, where it can be taken up by plants, or provide moisture for worms and other soil or-

ganisms. Our earth is the only place we know of where water is so common and readily available to support life.

Life requires numerous kinds of materials that our world supplies. Carbon is especially important because it can combine chemically in so many different ways. It turns out that carbon has some very special properties that could make it rare, but our world has enough carbon to support huge numbers of living organisms. Life also requires hydrogen, oxygen, phosophorus, nitrogen, sulfur, and small amounts of many other elements. Happily, these materials are available in our world. Many other materials are toxic to life, and, happily, these materials are rare in our world. The availability of needed materials and the rarity of toxic materials are necessary conditions for the survival of life, and one of the factors that makes our world special.

Conclusion

We live in a well-designed world, with exactly the right conditions for life. We are surrounded with living creatures with amazing abilities and interdependent relationships. These creatures exhibit an astounding diversity of shapes, colors, behaviors, and habitats. All these things suggest that there must have been a Creator who intended for the world to be an interesting and beautiful place.

Later, we will look at why we also see some ugliness in the world. But let's not forget how amazing and beautiful it is. In the next chapter, we will consider the marvelous abilities of humans—abilities that surprisingly have nothi .g to do with survival.

The Uniqueness
of Humans

Where were you on the evening of July 20, 1969? Did you stand outside and look up into the sky at the moon? A whole generation of humans—an estimated five hundred million people—watched on television as Neil Armstrong, Michael Collins, and Buzz Aldrin landed their lunar module, the *Eagle,* on the moon's Sea of Tranquility. As this historic event unfolded, as the first humans stood on the surface of the moon, there was no doubt that something dramatic and historically important was happening.

The plan to send men to the moon and return them safely to earth was announced by U.S. President John F. Kennedy in May 1961. He repeated the goal in a speech in September 1962. That speech became known as his "We choose to go to the moon" speech, which inspired millions to think big. Sending people to the moon and back was a big idea, and involved big risks. There was no guarantee of a safe ending to the story. To everyone's relief, the astronauts splashed down safely in the Pacific Ocean on July 24, and returned home in triumph. They

Astronaut
in space

45

were instant celebrities, having risked everything and succeeded in doing something that had never been done before.

As one would expect of such highly trained, professional men, the astronauts were quick to give credit for their success to the combined efforts of thousands of scientists and technicians. Their successful flight to the moon could not have been done by one or a few individuals. It required years of work by many thousands of highly trained professionals.

The uniqueness of humans

The success of the Apollo 11 mission was a spectacular accomplishment by humans. "Think Big" multi-year projects such as the Apollo missions are not uncommon in human societies, but they are unique to humans. No other species does such things. No other creatures carry out projects involving years of coordinated work by many individuals.

Apollo 11

Why not? Why couldn't they? Many other creatures have far greater populations, and some of them have amazing abilities that humans do not. Humans cannot fly like the birds, or swim like fish, or climb like monkeys. But humans can travel through the air or through

the water and reach any point in the trees because of their special abilities.

Humans can do things that make them different than other animals. They can accomplish wonderful things that no other creatures could do. Humans think up new ideas, create plans, prepare ahead of time for problems, and carry their plans forward to completion. The ability to plan, think, and accomplish new things—things that have never been done before—is a uniquely human trait.

Speech is another uniquely human trait that was necessary for the success of the moon flight. Many animal species can communicate, some of them in surprising ways. But none of them have the ability to speak like humans. Clear communication by speech is necessary for complex plans to be coordinated and completed. Speech and language make it possible for ideas to be shared, discussed, and evaluated. If humans were unable to speak, the Apollo project would never have been attempted, let alone completed.

Another thing unique about humans is the combination of self-consciousness and free will. As humans, we are able to recognize ourselves as individuals and to make decisions regarding how we will behave. This combination makes us responsible for our decisions. It gives us a sense of morality.

This moral sense motivates many people to behave responsibly and reliably, allowing us to cooperate on a scale far beyond anything simple animals can do. Thousands of human technicians were able to trust each other and cooperate for the good of the Apollo project, even when it inconvenienced them personally. Animals cannot accomplish such goals, in part because they lack the combination of self-consciousness and free will needed for a sense of

morality and responsibility.

Religion is another thing that is unique to humans. No other species could possibly have religious habits because they lack what is needed for morality—free will and self-consciousness. As strange as it may sound, you could argue that Christianity contributed to the success of the Apollo mission. How? Christianity provided the philosophical foundations—the thinking—necessary for the development of science. Science could not develop in a culture that thought nature was controlled by distant gods who were constantly fighting with each other and with humans, such as the Greek or Roman gods. No one could predict what would happen in nature any more than they could predict the mood of the gods.

Christianity taught that God was reliable and consistent in running the universe. So it made sense to try to discover the laws He used to run it. Christianity contributed to the success of science, including the Apollo mission, by providing a culture in which science could develop. Naturally, those who reject the idea of a God who is active in the universe disagree, but it's a point worthy of much discussion.[1]

> As humans, we are able to recognize ourselves as individuals and to make decisions regarding how we will behave.

Why humans are unique

It is clear that humans are unique among all the species on the earth. But why should this be true? Humans seem similar to other mammals—they have similar organs inside, they have arms and legs, they reproduce in similar ways. There certainly are similarities in their genes. So why are humans and animals so different? Two very different answers are usually given to this question: evolution and creation.

Evolutionary theory suggests that humans are simply advanced apes that have developed superior brains. Our language and speech, our self-consciousness, and our mechanical abilities are seen as simply improvements in

4—B.I.

things other species do. Many evolutionists would argue that humans don't really have free will and the morality that comes with it, even though it seems like we do.

There are a number of problems with this view. One of the most troubling problems is that evolutionary processes—which should exist only to ensure survival—do not explain why humans have abilities far beyond those needed just to survive. Why should humans appreciate art, music, and beauty? What evolutionary advantage is gained by the ability to paint a picture, or to compose a poem, or to enjoy the flowers? There are many similar objections that could be made. To many, they show that evolutionary theory is not a good explanation for the extraordinary abilities of humans.

What if humans were created by a Being with powers beyond our understanding? Could that explain why we have these kinds of abilities? Let's take some time to explore the Christian story of creation and see.

The Bible book of Genesis describes the creation of humans this way:

1. They were created out of the dirt—this is, out of the same carbon-based building blocks as every other kind of life on earth.
2. They were created in two forms—male and female. With complementary parts and organs, they were created with the ability to reproduce, to create new humans in the form of babies.
3. They were created in the image of God—that is, in some way, their abilities were a reflection of God's abilities.

There is no question that the first two parts of the Bible's Creation story are accurate. Humans are carbon-based life forms, just as all life on earth is carbon-based. And humans can reproduce, re-creating human babies in every new generation. But if the third part of the Creation story is accurate, what would that mean?

The image of God

If humans were unique in being created in "the image of God," then it makes sense that we would have abilities that other animals do not. How do our unique abilities compare to what the Bible tells us about God?

What about relationships? If God created humans in both male and female form, then God's image must be best seen in a relationship between the two. The Bible describes God as a being of relationships, Someone who wants to be in a relationship with humans. Like God, we are beings of relationships. We live in families, in communities, in nations, and everything we do is focused on how we are relating to others.

The human ability to have relationships with others may be a reflection of one part of the image of God.

As we discovered earlier, human creativity goes far beyond anything needed just to survive. This creativity allows humans to solve many complex problems, such as sending a man to the moon. Many other spectacular examples could be given of human creativity in problem-solving, but there is more to the story. We can find solutions to difficult problems, but with our creativity, we also explore things not needed for survival—things like beauty.

> The human ability to have relationships with others may be a reflection of one part of the image of God.

If God created our world, then He must also be a lover of beauty. Humans have created colorful paintings, dramatic sculptures, magnificent buildings and bridges, and many kinds of music. But these only faintly imitate the beauty in sunsets and flowers, in natural landscapes, and in the sounds of birds and other creatures. Can it be that humans love beauty because they were created in the image of a God who loves beauty?

If humans were created by God, then that may explain why we have abilities to think creatively, to plan ahead,

and to appreciate beauty. It may explain why humans have self-consciousness and free will. It may explain why we can speak and understand language. It may explain why relationships are so important to us.

Human responsibilities

In the Creation story of Genesis, God gives humans a job. They are assigned to manage the resources of the earth. God creates the earth, and humans are to take care of it (read about it in Genesis 1:28).

First, humans are given the responsibility to "multiply," to produce children and expand the population. This means establishing families and communities. The family is the basic building block of society. If God is a Being of relationships, then reflecting His image means building strong families.

Then, as they fill the earth with larger populations, humans are asked to manage the resources of the planet. If God's image is reflected in them, they will treat the creatures of earth with kindness and safeguard the environment that all creatures share.

No one could claim that humans have managed the resources of the earth properly—not the way we have polluted the skies and water by the overuse of coal and oil. Not the way we've hunted some animals to extinction and allowed others to be wiped out by destroying their habitats. Too often, we've chosen profits and greed instead of responsible planning for the future.

But we could have—and we could still. We have the abilities to manage the earth, and those abilities—to reason from cause to effect, to creatively plan ahead and work in cooperation—are far beyond what we would need to simply survive. Caring for the creation requires the very abilities that are unique to humans—the kind you would see if humans were created "in the image of God."

Conclusion

Humans are unique! And the Bible's Creation story could explain why. It has an answer for why humans have abilities beyond the need for survival. And it tells what might be the purpose of these special abilities.

Do our special abilities reflect the "image of God"? Is our ability to form relationships and our creativity just a result of an accident? Did our love of beauty, our complex language skills, our abstract thinking, and our free will just happen without cause? It seems unimaginable that the very things that make us human are only a result of random chance.

Let's continue this journey of discovery and try to focus in on the questions for which science has no answers: Why are we here? And where are we going?

> Humans are unique! And the Bible's Creation story could explain why.

---

1. Numerous scholars have affirmed the importance of Christian belief in a rational, consistent God as a necessary precondition for the development of science. For example, see S.L. Jaki, *Science and Creation* (Edinburgh: Scottish Academic Press, 1974); Loren Eiseley, *Darwin's Century* (Garden City, N.Y.: Anchor Doubleday, 1961), 62; Dan Graves, *Scientists of Faith* (Grand Rapids, Mich.: Kregel Resources, 1996).

A Gift of
Balance

The wonders of this universe are too amazing to be accidental. The creatures of our planet are too remarkable to have appeared by chance. Our own abilities are more developed than evolution can explain.

All of this points to a Creator who gave special abilities—and special responsibilities—to humans. The Creation story in Genesis suggests that God gave humans responsibilities to care for the earth and the life on it. He set us up as caretakers for the rest of His creation. And since we would need to depend on Him and on each other, He created beings who must live in relationship with each other.

Besides the special abilities given to humans who were made in the "image of God," another gift was given in the Creation story in Genesis. It says that "on the seventh day God ended His work which He had done, and He rested on the seventh day from all His work which He had done" (Genesis 2:2).

It's hard to suggest that the God who created the vast universe would have been exhausted by creating our small planet. Even though we can't even imagine what it means to "create," it doesn't seem like the sort of work that would cause someone to break a sweat or need a break.

Rest

So why would God rest? And why was it important to include this announcement of "rest" in the story? Could it

be that this seventh day of rest is not in the story for God, but for humans? Maybe by imitating God's pattern of six days of creative work and a seventh day devoted to relationships, we are expressing an important aspect of God's image. Is it possible that when we follow this divine example, we escape the trap of focusing only on surviving—or as we see it today, on making a living?

Think about it. What a wonderful gift that would be! Did God know, for example, that:

- Our problem-solving skills could lead us to work too many hours when the solution didn't come easily?

- Our creativity would push us to stay up too late and not get enough rest?
- Our self-awareness would lead us to second-guess all our decisions, creating high stress?

Maybe God knew that we would need a time-out every week to recover from the stress of everyday life. Maybe He knew that our relationships would suffer if we didn't have a built-in reason to stop and dedicate time to them.

If we have one day each week to focus on rest and relationships, we improve our lives in three different ways:

First, we have time to pursue a relationship with our Creator. Amazingly, a Being as unimaginably powerful and creative as He must be, still is focused on relationships—including relationships with humans like us.

> Maybe God knew that our relationships would suffer if we didn't have a built-in reason to stop and dedicate time to them.

Second, our weekly "Sabbath" rest is a time to build social relationships—our connection to those around us. The Sabbath was made for humans, Jesus said, and worshiping on Sabbath includes time with family and time in church.

Finally, Sabbath is a wonderful time for a relationship with the rest of the creation. Spending time in the outdoors gives us an opportunity to rest and recuperate away from the b_syness and noise of our daily lives.

What difference does it make?

The Creation story says that God rested on the seventh day. But could it possibly matter which day we rest? What difference does a day make? Surely what matters is setting the time aside for relationship and worship.

Let's answer that by looking at a story from the Bible book of 2 Kings. Naaman was a commander in the army of ancient Syria (also called Aram) when he contracted one of the most dreaded diseases of the day—leprosy. Not only was leprosy a death sentence; it was a slow and horrible death. (Leprosy is still present in some parts of the world today, but there is effective treatment.)

The disease causes sores on the skin and damage to nerves. In those days, with no treatment available, it led to deformed hands and feet, as well as horrible skin growths. And if the disease wasn't bad enough, anyone with leprosy was considered "unclean" or contagious. They had to separate themselves from their family and friends and either live alone or with other lepers. It was not just a physical death sentence—it was a social death sentence and seen as a punishment of the gods.

> The Creation story says that God rested on the seventh day.

Naaman, a powerful and important leader in the army, was desperate to find some cure before others became aware of his disease and shunned him.

Syrian ruins

At that time, Syria was one of the dominant nations in the area and although open war had not been declared with the Israelites (also called Hebrews), there were ongoing raids on the Hebrew towns. In fact, there was a Hebrew slave girl working in Naaman's home as his wife's maid. Naaman's wife must have treated her well because when she heard about the disease, she said, "If only master Naaman could see the prophet in Samaria. He can cure leprosy."

Samaria was the capital of Israel, deep inside enemy territory! But Naaman was desperate, so he went to his king and requested permission to visit Samaria. The king didn't want to lose such a valuable military leader. So he sent a letter—and a great deal of gold and silver—to King Joram of Israel saying, "I am sending my servant to you. Please have him healed."

King Joram knew that leprosy was incurable. He could only see a plot. *This Syrian king just wants to blame me when Naaman dies. Then he'll attack us with his army!* He stood up and ripped his robe. "Am I God to decide who lives or dies?" he shouted.

Naaman was ready to give up and go home, but the prophet Elisha heard what the king had done. He sent a message saying, "Why are you so upset? Send the man to me and the Syrians will learn that there is a real prophet in Israel."

Jordan River

When Naaman and his entourage arrived at Elisha's house, he expected the prophet to perform a healing ritual or make a sacrifice to the gods. But Elisha's servant Gehazi appeared at the door alone. He passed on Elisha's instruction: "Go and wash yourself in the Jordan River seven times. Then you will be healed."

"What?!" Naaman was already mad that the prophet hadn't even bothered to step outside and meet him. Instead, Elisha orders him to wash in a dirty river! "If washing would do any good, why wouldn't I wash in the rivers of Syria?" Then he stomped off and headed for home.

Naaman was asking, "What difference does a river make?" Water is water, so why should it matter? If Elisha's God wants me to dip in water, then it's the dipping that counts, not the river in which I dip. But there was something Naaman didn't know.

"Master," one of Naaman's servants called, "if the prophet had asked you to do something difficult or dangerous, you would have done it. Can it hurt to try dipping in the Jordan River?"

So Naaman turned toward the river and did as Elisha instructed. Seven times he dipped himself under the water and when he rose up the last time, his leprosy was gone!

Why did it matter which river Naaman dipped in? First, it was a test to show whether or not he really believed in Elisha and the power of Elisha's God. Second, there was something different in the Jordan River—something that wasn't in the rivers of Syria (see 2 Kings 5).

> "What difference does a river make?" Water is water, so why should it matter?

Stones of blessing

Several hundred years before Naaman's time, when the Hebrews who escaped from Egypt finally made it to the land of Canaan, they were stopped by the Jordan River. The river was flooding and there was no way to cross. According to the Bible book of Joshua, God commanded that the priests who were carrying the sacred ark of the covenant to wade out and stand in the middle of the river.

When they did, the flow of the water stopped! As the priests stood in place, the north end of the river piled up

River stones

behind them as the south end flowed away and dried out. After all the people had crossed, God directed them to stack twelve river stones at the spot where they had crossed. It was an endless reminder that their God—their Creator God—had touched the waters of the Jordan River and opened the way for them. Those stones are still there today.

The water of the Jordan River did have a special blessing that the rivers of Syria didn't have. God had touched that water in a special way many years before. It wasn't the water or the rocks that healed Naaman, but the blessing of the Creator whom Elisha worshiped.

A special day

Now back to our question: If God gave us a gift—one day in seven to rest—because of the other special gifts we have, does it matter which day we rest, which day we worship on?

The seventh day is special for two reasons:

First, the Creation story says, "the seventh day." Like the story of Naaman that doesn't say, "Dip in a river, any river will do," it doesn't say, "God rested on a day, any day." It says "the seventh day."

The Bible's Ten Commandments in the book of Exodus chapter 20 make it even more specific. It says, "Six days you shall labor and do all your work, but the seventh day is the Sabbath of the LORD your God. . . . For in six days the LORD made the heavens and the earth, the sea, and all that is in them, and rested the seventh day. Therefore the LORD blessed the Sabbath day and hallowed it."

When Naaman dipped himself in the Jordan River, he showed that he believed in Elisha's God. When humans rest on the seventh day, we show that we believe in the God of creation.

Second, like the Jordan River was blessed by the touch of God when the Hebrews crossed over, the seventh day was blessed by the touch of the Creator. There is a special blessing for those who keep it, just as there was a special blessing for Naaman in the waters of the Jordan River.

In the Creation story, the rest on the seventh day is just as much a part of the record as is the creation of birds on the

> When humans rest on the seventh day, we show that we believe in the God of creation.

fifth day or the animals on the sixth day. The Sabbath rest was part of a package of gifts given to humans. Humans

were given responsibilities that would cause stress, and problem-solving skills that would bring pressure. But in the same act of creation that brought them into being, they were given a counter-balance, a gift that could off-set the problems those gifts might bring.

Conclusion

There's no doubt that humans are different than other species on earth. If we are more than just advanced apes, more than just smart monkeys, then maybe we are part of a plan to fill the earth with life and care for it. If we were

created "in the image" of the God who created the universe, what does it mean?

The wonders of the universe are beyond imagination. Is it possible that a Being with that kind of power cares about humans? That a Creator God gave us special gifts like self-awareness and creativity? And that He gave us a gift of time off to keep those gifts in balance?

But there are still questions that need to be answered. If God created our world, and if He cares about humans, then why do so many bad things happen to us? Why is there pain and suffering in the world?

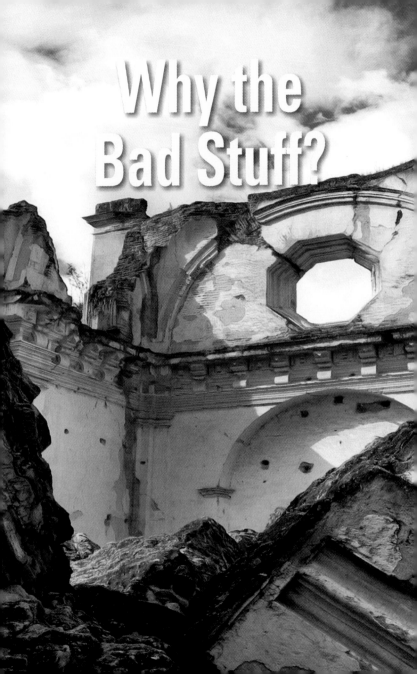

Why the Bad Stuff?

CHAPTER 6

November 1, 1755, was an important religious holiday in Portugal. Normally King Joseph I and his queen Mariana Victoria of Spain would join the great crowds and attend a midmorning worship service at one of the large churches. But one of their daughters wanted to spend the holiday at the coast. It was a beautiful day, so the king agreed. The family went to a service at dawn, then left their royal Ribeira Palace on the bank of the Tagus River to enjoy a day in the countryside, little knowing they would never see their home again.

About 9:40 that morning, a section of sea floor ruptured off the coast of Portugal, producing one of the largest earthquakes in recorded history, with an estimated magnitude of 8.5 to 9.0 on the Richter scale. The records of the day suggest that there were three distinct quakes within a span of ten minutes, the second shock being the strongest. While many of the details were lost over time, there is no doubt that the Great Lisbon Earthquake of 1755 was one of the most significant natural disasters in history.

Records show that the shaking was felt from Finland to Africa, and tsunamis of various sizes struck North Africa, France, England, Ireland, Belgium, Holland, and the islands of the Caribbean.

The earthquake destroyed much of the city of Lisbon, including the royal palace with its library of some seventy thousand volumes, the king's cathedral, and a priceless art collection. The churches, full of worshipers, collapsed, killing many hundreds of people. Thousands of homes and other buildings were destroyed or damaged, and crowds of survivors ran out of doors to safety, gathering around the docks where there were no buildings to collapse upon them. From the docks, they could watch the water of the bay recede out to sea, exposing lost ship-

wrecks and assorted items of lost cargo. Not realizing the danger they were in, many ran out to search for treasure in the sunken ships.

Unknown to the crowd, the quakes would be followed by a series of three tsunamis. The water first pushed westward, emptying the bay. A few minutes later, a tsunami wave twenty to thirty feet high, crashed up the Tagus River into the city, destroying what remained of the buildings that were located close to the water. The docks and all the ships in the harbor were demolished, and thousands of people who had survived the earthquake were lost to the tsunamis. Horrible as this was, there was more to follow.

Many people had left their homes in such a hurry that they did not put out their cooking fires, and candles had been burning in every church for the holiday. Soon, fire began to spread through the city, aided by looters wishing to hide the evidence of their thievery. The fire destroyed much of what the earthquake and tsunami left. Fires burned out of control for five or six days. The All Saints Royal Hospital, the largest in the city, burned to the ground, killing hundreds of patients.

> Because of the excellent sailing skills of the Portuguese explorers and traders, Lisbon was one of the richest cities of its day.

The royal family survived the disaster, but King Joseph I was never willing to live inside a walled building again. The entire royal court was moved to a giant tented complex outside of Lisbon where he lived until his death.[1]

A turning point

Lisbon was the fourth largest city in Europe at the time of the earthquake, with a population estimated at about 200,000 to 250,000. Because of the excellent sailing skills of the Portuguese explorers and traders, it was one of the richest cities of its day.

But the earthquake changed everything. Between the quake, the tsunamis, and the fires, thirty thousand to forty thousand people were killed and 75 to 85 percent of the city was destroyed. Portugal lost much of its political and economic power, and that was never recovered. But more importantly to us, the event also marked a turning point in the way people thought.

Before the earthquake, people in Europe had a very idealistic way of looking at religion and the world. Some European philosophers thought that the world was just as God had created it—the best of all possible worlds. Other leading thinkers had their doubts. The earthquake seemed to settle the question: this was clearly not the best possible world.

> The Lisbon earthquake led to a major change in European thinking culture.

From a religious point of view, there didn't seem to be any reason for the terrible Lisbon catastrophe of 1755. Some church leaders insisted that the earthquake was some kind of divine punishment on the city. But others pointed out that the red-light district—the seedy section where prostitutes, drugs, and strong drink was available at every corner—was only lightly damaged, while most of the major churches and cathedrals were destroyed. That didn't fit well with the idea that God had sent punishment.

People began to search for other ways to understand their world. The Lisbon earthquake led to a major change in European thinking culture. Catastrophes came to be seen to be the results of natural forces rather than divine judgments. God seemed to be distant and uninvolved, and scientists became more interested in searching for the natural reasons why earthquakes, storms, droughts, and other disasters happened.

The problem of evil

We may not experience something as dramatic or catastrophic as the Great Lisbon Earthquake, but one thing is the same in all of our lives: bad things happen.

Some of us face diseases such as cancer or hepatitis. Some deal with crippling injuries or birth defects. Traffic accidents can happen in the blink of an eye. We see reports of storms, wars, and crimes taking lives every day. Where does all this suffering and sadness come from? Why do these things happen?

We've talked about the wonders of the universe and the power of a God who could create such things. But where is this God when people are suffering? Why does God let evil things happen to us?

If God created such a wonderful world for us, where did it all go wrong?

Curse God and die

The Bible book of Job tells a story of a very rich and religious man named Job. He has a wife, seven sons, and three daughters. His fields are full of oxen, donkeys, camels, and sheep. He is a faithful follower of God, and he is blessed with wealth and happiness.

But then the story shifts to an unusual point of view—the courts of God Himself. There a meeting is taking place. All the "sons of God" have been called together and with them is "the adversary"—or as we usually translate it—Satan. And Satan has been walking among God's children on earth.

"Did you meet My servant, Job?" God asks. "He is a good man, a faithful follower."

Satan snorted. "Of course he's faithful—You've given him everything he could possibly want and protected him from any evil. Take away all he treasures, and he will curse You!"

"OK," God says. "Let's see if you are right. Do anything you want to Job—just don't touch him."

And so it happened: disasters of all kinds struck quickly. Job's oxen, donkeys, and camels were stolen by raiders. Fire fell from the sky and killed all his sheep. Then a storm knocked down the house when his children were eating, killing them all. In one day, everything Job held dear was gone.

Did he blame God when these terrible things happened? No. Job shaved his head, tore his clothes, and said, "The LORD gave, and the LORD has taken away; blessed be the name of the LORD" (Job 1:21).

> All the "sons of God" have been called together and with them is "the adversary."

This time, when God questions Satan about Job's faithfulness, Satan says, "A man will do anything You want as long as You protect his health. Take that away and he will curse You."

Again, God agrees to a test. "Do whatever you want to his body, but don't take his life."

Now Satan struck Job with terrible sores from the top of his head to the soles of his feet. As Job was sitting in ashes (this showed his sorrow), scraping at his sores with a broken piece of pottery, his wife said, "What else can happen to you? Just curse God and die already!"

"No," Job said. "We take the good things when God gives them to us. Shouldn't we also take the bad?"

Then Job is joined by friends who first try to comfort him, then try to convince him that he has clearly sinned and offended God. Why else would he be punished so severely?

But Job will not agree. "I have done nothing wrong," he insists. But he does wish that he had never been born and begs God to explain why these terrible things have happened.

Why do bad things happen in a world that God created?

When God finally speaks to Job, it is out of a mighty whirlwind. "Where were you, Job, when I created the earth? Are you stronger than a storm or the mighty creatures of the earth?"

God doesn't answer Job's questions. He seems to say, "You don't know enough to understand these issues. You can't understand—you have to trust Me."

And that is what Job does. He is sorry that he ever doubted God and promises to trust Him.

The story ends with God blessing Job again and giving him more than he ever had before. He has a new family of children, and lives long enough to see four generations of grandchildren.

Behind the scenes

Why do bad things happen in a world that God created? We can learn several things from the story of Job.

1. The bad things that happen to us are not caused by God.
2. There is something going on behind the scenes of the world we live in, something we can't see.
3. Some things that happen don't have an explanation that humans can understand.

Let's go back to the Creation story in the Bible. The first chapter of Genesis tells about the perfect world God is creating. Humans are placed in a beautiful garden paradise in chapter 2, and given the job of naming all the creatures. Adam and Eve are told that they can eat the fruit of any tree in the Garden, except one. This one is identified as "the tree of the knowledge of good and evil." The two humans are told to stay away from it.

But in chapter 3, Eve apparently strays too close to the tree, and hears an enticing voice. "Did God tell you not to eat this fruit?"

It was a snake, speaking to her from the tree. "God said that we can eat the fruit of any tree in the Garden except this one," she answered. "If we eat it, we will die."

"Of course you won't die," said the snake. "God just knows that if you eat this fruit, you'll become like Him, knowing good and evil."

Eve was faced with a choice—trust God and obey Him, or take a chance with the snake. Eve chose to eat the fruit, and Adam joined her in disobeying God. That's when everything changed—because behind the scenes, something else was happening.

Fallen from heaven

In the book of Ezekiel, the Bible tells about an angel who went bad. "You were the anointed cherub. . . . You were perfect in your ways from the day you were created, Till iniquity was found in you" (Ezekiel 28:14, 15). This angel is called Lucifer in some places, but in the Bible book of Luke, Jesus says, "I saw Satan fall like lightning from heaven" (Luke 10:18).

This fallen angel is the adversary from the story of Job, the one who accuses humans of not being faithful. This fallen angel is the one who speaks to Eve through the snake in the Garden.

Behind the scenes of human history, a whole different drama is being played out. Lucifer, an angel of heaven, rebelled against God. He wanted to be in charge instead of God. The typical human response to rebellion is to destroy the rebel. So why didn't God do that?

One answer might be that God couldn't, that He didn't have the power to destroy Lucifer. But according to the story, God created Lucifer—

as well as the rest of the universe—so it certainly seems like destroying him would be no difficulty.

The price of freedom

The answer might go back to what we learned about God and the special gifts He gave humans. If God gave humans the gift of free will, it could only be because He wanted them to be free to exercise that will. If God wanted creatures who always obeyed without question, who always followed every rule exactly, He could have created robots. Take away the freedom to choose, and you take away the possibility of making wrong, painful choices.

> The typical human response to rebellion is to destroy the rebel. So why didn't God do that?

But without free will, you can't have relationships. With the proper threat or bribe, you can get someone to spend time with you. But if they don't "choose" to be your friend, then you have no real relationship with them.

If we suppose that God also created the angels with freedom to choose, that He also wanted to have real relationships with them, then we can see that Lucifer was free to rebel against God. And what would be the result if God just destroyed Lucifer for rebelling?

Everyone else would obey God out of fear—fear of what He would do to them if they stepped out of line. Freedom would be lost.

So God expelled Lucifer from heaven—to our earth. Now he is known as the adversary, Satan. And in the Garden, Satan was the one tempting Eve to doubt God. He was tempting Eve to join in his rebellion against God.

When the humans chose to join the rebellion against God, everything changed. God had warned them that eating the fruit would cause death, and it did. From that

moment on, death was a part of life on our earth. From that moment on, Adam and Eve began to age and die.

Instead of only roses, now there were thorns. Instead of only flowers or vegetable plants, now there were weeds. Instead of long life and health, there was sickness and pain and death.

Conclusion

What could God do? Was there no way to preserve freedom, but still stop the endless cycle of pain and death?

There was a way. A plan. We will explore that in the next chapter.

---

1. http://www.lisbonweekendguild.com/Lisbon-information/1755_lisbon_earthquake_2.html.

The Jesus
Plan

Chapter 7

Imagine that you are walking down the side-walk of a busy city street, holding the hand of a child you love. "See those cars racing by?" you say. "Don't walk out there where they are. Stay with me on the sidewalk and you'll be safe."

You keep walking, stepping around delivery carts, dodging people with packages, and hopping over puddles. Then you pass the opening of a dark alleyway. "See that alley?" you say as you point. "Don't go down there. There may be dangerous people there, people who would hurt you. Stay here on the sidewalk with me."

As you walk, the child lets go of your hand several times to step over and stare into store windows or at an interesting bug on the ground. Then a bird lands on the ground nearby and the child lets go of your hand to step toward it. You have to step back to avoid a man carrying boxes, and you see the bird hop toward an alley opening. The child follows it. "Wait," you call out, "don't go that way."

But you're forced to step back again to avoid a woman on a bicycle. You see the bird disappear down the alleyway with the child right behind it. "No!" you shout. You race to the alley as quickly as you can, but the child is nowhere to be seen. You race down the dark passageway, shouting the child's name as you go. You search behind every dumpster, overturn every box, rattle every locked door.

> When Adam and Eve chose to join Satan's rebellion, they were on a path that would lead to pain, sadness, and death.

You race around one more corner and slide to a stop. The child stands against a chain link fence. Between you is a gang of street thugs. One slaps a bat across his palm. Another flicks a knife open and closed. The one with a whirling chain steps toward the child.

What do you do? You could:

- Turn and walk away. After all, you warned the child not to go into the alley.
- Call for help, then wait to see what happens.
- Shout at the thugs to leave the child alone and hope that works.
- Run to rescue the child. Even if it costs your life.

What would you do?
Let me tell you the story of Jesus.

A rescue mission

Most of us have heard the story of Baby Jesus. At Christmastime, we hear songs about a baby born in a manger, about angels singing and wise men visiting. But the story of Jesus really begins long before that. Back in the Creation story, where we saw that humans were created in the "image of God," notice what is actually said: "Then God said, 'Let Us make man in Our image, according to Our likeness . . .' " (Genesis 1:26).

Who is God talking to? Who is the "Us"? Because of what is said in other places in the Bible, Christians believe that Jesus was there at Creation, that He was with God; that He was God. In fact, most Christians believe Jesus was the Creator of earth. When His followers asked about God, Jesus taught them about His "Father." So God the Father and Jesus were both at Creation.

As we saw in the last chapter, there was a rebellion in heaven. When Satan was thrown out, he came to earth. God knew that if humans were going to have free will, then they would have to choose whether to trust Him or listen to Satan. When Adam and Eve chose to join Satan's rebellion, they were on a path that would lead to pain, sadness, and death. And not just them, but their children and grandchildren, and all their descendants. Humans had wandered off the sidewalk and down the alley, and now they were faced with tragedy and death.

Just as you had options in the story above, God and Jesus had options when humans rebelled. Just as They could have done with Lucifer, They could have wiped out humans and started over. But that choice would show that there was no real freedom.

They could have stood back and let humans suffer and fight and kill until they were extinct. They could have pointed to humans as an example for the rest of the universe: "See what happens when you choose to rebel?" But that choice would have shown how little their relationship to humans meant—it would have shown no real love.

Instead, they chose a rescue mission—*a five-part rescue mission.* This wouldn't be quick or easy, but it would be permanent when it was done.

Part one—the promise. Before they even left the Garden to begin their difficult lives in a world of thorns and hard work, danger and death, Adam and Eve heard God curse the snake and promise that one of Eve's children would crush him (Genesis 3:15). All through the first part of the Bible—the history of the Hebrew people as they struggled to be faithful followers—God gave promises that someone was coming to rescue them from their troubles, to save them from sin and death.

> But the real rescue plan took everyone by surprise. Jesus Himself came to earth!

As the Hebrews fought with other tribes and nations for territory and control of their Promised Land, they prayed for a mighty warrior to save them. Later, when Israel, the land of the Hebrews (or Jews, as they are known now), was controlled by the great armies of Greece and then Rome, they prayed for a great king of their own who would set them free.

Part two—the surprise. But the real rescue plan took everyone by surprise. Jesus Himself came to earth! By some power beyond our imagination, He was born as a human baby. He would grow up human, live as a human, and show that a human could follow God faithfully.

His life started out like anyone else's in that day. He lived at home, went to school and worked in the family business. But when the time was right, He left home and began to teach people about God. The things He said about God were very different than what other teachers and church leaders were saying.

> Jesus traveled through the countryside, teaching whoever would listen.

- The teachers of the day said that following God means following a very strict lifestyle. Jesus said that following God means taking care of the poor and those in need.
- The teachers said that God wants to destroy our enemies. Jesus said that we should love our enemies.
- They said that God takes care of the good people but hates the bad people. Jesus taught that God loves each of us and that we should love each other.

As Jesus traveled through the countryside, teaching whoever would listen, the crowds that followed Him grew larger and larger. There are many stories of Him healing sick people, curing blindness—He even healed people who had leprosy like Naaman!

The Bible book of Mark tells the story of a man from the town of Capernaum who was paralyzed. He had been to doctors and priests, but they said he was incurable and cursed by God. Then he heard about Jesus. With one last shred of hope, he asked his friends to carry him to where Jesus was teaching.

On that day, Jesus was teaching inside a house. His

disciples were sitting around their Master listening, and nearby were a number of religious leaders who had come to spy on Jesus. Outside was an enormous crowd who had come to listen through the open windows and watch to see if Jesus did any more miracles.

The paralyzed man's friends tried to push their way through the crowd as they carried him on a stretcher, but they couldn't. Just as they gave up hope of getting to Jesus, the man had an idea. "Carry me up to the roof," he suggested. "We can go through from there."

So that's what they did. In those days, most homes in Capernaum had roofs made of woven grass or palm fronds. The man's friends carried him up on top of the house, then broke through and lowered his stretcher down until he was lying at Jesus' feet.

When Jesus saw the man's pleading eyes, He knew exactly what to say. "Son, your sins are forgiven."

These words were music to the paralyzed man's ears. His depression and pain were gone. More than just healed, he was forgiven!

The religious leaders who were there were sure that the paralyzed man was cursed by God and Jesus was doing a terrible thing. "Who does this Jesus think he is? God? This is a sin worthy of death!" they said to themselves.

But Jesus was reading their faces and hearts. "Why are you thinking like that among yourselves?" He asked. "Which is easier, to say to this paralyzed man, 'You are forgiven,' or to say, 'Stand, pick up your stretcher and walk'? But so you will know that I have the authority to forgive sins, I will tell you." He said to the paralyzed man, "Stand, pick up your stretcher and go home."

> Jesus was the way out of the trap humans had fallen into by joining Satan's rebellion.

This was the same Voice heard at Creation. Now it recreated the body of a forgiven man. He jumped up from the floor as frisky as a growing boy. With new, strong muscles, he picked up the stretcher like it weighed no more than a feather and walked out through the crowd.

The people stepped back to give him room and whispered to each other, "We have seen strange and wonderful things today" (see Mark 2).

So many of the things Jesus said seemed strange and wonderful. He said two things were most important for anyone who wanted to follow His way: " 'You shall love the Lord your God with all your heart, with all your soul, and with all your mind.' This is the first and great commandment. And the second is like it: 'You shall love your neighbor as yourself' " (Matthew 22:37–39).

He also taught something so simple but so powerful that it can solve problems in personal relationships, in families, and even in communities. Jesus described it as a simple expression of everything the Bible teaches. He said, "Do to others what you want them to do to you" (see Matthew 7:12).

Treat other people the way we want to be treated! What would the world look like if we all did that?

Part three—the payment. Jesus' love as He lived among humans brought joy and peace to them, but there was still a price to be paid. Jesus was the way out of the trap humans had fallen into by joining Satan's rebellion. He promised that by believing in Him and following His way, they could escape sin and live with Him forever, just as Adam and Eve were meant to do. But Jesus didn't just use words to promise. He threw His body over us to save us.

Jesus' life on earth ended when He was arrested by the Jewish religious leaders. They hated Him because the people were following Him instead of listening to them. They told the Romans that Jesus was claiming to be the King of the Jews, and the Romans sent Him to be crucified—hung on a cross of wood until He was dead. Remember, now, that

Jesus was God—He could have stopped them at any time. But He didn't. The Bible story of the crucifixion of Jesus says that the skies turned dark in the middle of the afternoon. It was as if God the Father couldn't bear to watch. But He didn't stop the Romans either.

Jesus died on the cross to pay for the rebellious sins of humans.

This was the payment for the plan to save humans. At Creation, when God told Adam and Eve that they would die if they ate the fruit, He meant that they would die forever—they would be cut off from the Creator of life. When Adam and Eve ate the fruit, God the Father and Jesus set the plan in motion: humans couldn't live forever while they rebelled, so they aged and died. But if Jesus came and died for all humans, then those who chose to follow His way could once again live forever with God.

Part four—the resurrection. Jesus died on the cross to pay for the rebellious sins of humans. But He was never in rebellion against God. He hadn't committed any sins. So on the third day after He was buried, He rose up from the grave! And He said to His followers, "I am the resurrection and the life. He who believes in Me, though he may die, he shall live" (John 11:25).

All those who believed in God, who followed His path, all the way back to Adam and Eve—all could be resurrected and live again with Jesus in heaven. He promised, "In My Father's house are many mansions; if it were not so, I would have told you. I go to prepare a place for you" (John 14:2).

That was the rescue plan. Adam and Eve got all humans into sin and the rebellion against God. Jesus gave all humans a way out.

Conclusion

When His human children got lost in rebellion, the Creator God didn't abandon them or wipe them out and start over. He launched a plan to rescue them. Jesus came to show humans what God was really like and to pay the price to bring them back to God.

What about *part five* of the rescue plan? That's what we'll discover in the next chapter.

Rescue
From Above

The miners who worked Chile's San Jose copper-gold mine felt the weight of the stone above them every day as they descended down the spiral entrance ramp into the darkness. More than one hundred years old, the mine often groaned and rained dust on them as they swung their picks and worked their machines. With a number of previous accidents, the facility had paid multiple fines for safety violations. But work is work, so every day men entered the mine, trusting that the rocks around them would hold in place for one more shift.

August 5, 2010, seemed like any other day for the thirty-three men working deep in the mine. Then with a sharp crack, about seven hundred thousand tons of rock shifted, cutting off the ramps and destroying the ventilation shaft. They were trapped 2,300 feet underground and about three miles from the mine's entrance.

It didn't take the miners long to realize that they had no way to escape—they could only hope for rescue from above.

Many felt that there was no way for the men to have survived, but the Chilean people refused

Chilean "paloma" supply tube

95

to give up hope. Under much public pressure, the government took over the search and rescue operation and eight boreholes were quickly drilled toward the space it was thought the miners might be. Seventeen days after the accident, a drill-bit that had broken through to an empty chamber was pulled up carrying a note: *"Estamos bien en el refugio, los 33"* ("We are well in the shelter, the 33 of us").

Overwhelmed with joy, the people of Chile demanded that a way be found to rescue the trapped workers.

Food, water, and medical supplies were sent down to the men in "palomas," supply tubes, especially designed to fit down the narrow drill holes. Video and phone lines were also set up, so the men below could communicate with the rescuers and with their families.

Then the real rescue work began. The Chilean government organized the efforts of their own people as well as experts from more than a dozen mining corporations around the world. Three large international drilling rig teams went to work boring a hole large enough to fit a human. Finally, after sixty-nine dark days deep underground, all thirty-three men were rescued. It is estimated that more than one billion people watched the rescue live on television or over the Internet.

Part five—the rescue

In the Bible's Creation story, we saw how quickly the beauty and peace of the earth turned bad. When humans joined the rebellion against God, they were all trapped in a world filled with sin—filled with anger, fear, danger, sickness, and death. Just like the Chilean miners, they were trapped with no way of saving themselves. Their only hope was rescue from above.

Jesus' five-part rescue mission began with promises and prophecies. And part five begins with the same. When Jesus was on earth with His followers, He talked about the day when the rescue would happen—when He would put an end to the rebellion and save all those who followed Him.

> The Bible has many promises and prophecies about Jesus' return.

He said, "I go to prepare a place for you. And if I go and prepare a place for you, I will come again and receive you to Myself; that where I am, there you may be also" (John 14:2, 3).

The Bible has many promises and prophecies about Jesus' return. It's also called "the end of the world" or "the end of time," since that is when Jesus puts an end to everything that has gone wrong since Creation. When Jesus' followers asked Him how they would know when the end was near, He gave them some signs to watch for. He said:

- Others would claim to be the one who would save them.
- Wars and famine will happen, and many earthquakes.

- Believers will be hated, arrested, and killed.
- False prophets will tell lies, and evil, hate, and sin would be everywhere.
- Good news about God's kingdom will be shared with the whole world. And then the end will come.

Have we seen any of these things happen? The world has seen many spiritual leaders such as Sun Myung Moon of the Unification Church who have claimed to be the one who would save their followers. Others, such as David Koresh of the Branch Davidians, have led their followers to their deaths.

> Everywhere we turn are people claiming to speak in God's name, twisting the words of the Bible to agree with their hateful and angry messages.

War has been a part of human history from the beginning, but only in recent times have we had wars that include most of the nations on earth, such as World War II. Today, wars may be limited to smaller areas, but we have developed weapons that can kill millions and destroy vast areas of the planet.

Often made worse by war that keeps help from the people who need it most, famine continues to plague our world. Too many places face starvation when there could be enough food to feed every hungry child.

The great earthquake in Lisbon in 1755 was only the beginning. They seem to come more often and do more damage than ever before. The 2004 earthquake and tsunami in the Indian Ocean may have been the most deadly in human history, killing more than 150 thousand people. More recently, the 2011 earthquake and tsunami in Japan killed many thousands more and devastated a large area of that country.

In some places today, people who believe in Jesus are arrested and even beaten or killed. Many faithful people have to worship in secret and share their faith with great risk. But that isn't the case in most of the world. Jesus seems to be saying that this will happen more and more as we get closer to the end.

Are there false prophets telling lies today? Everywhere we turn are people claiming to speak in God's name, twisting the words of the Bible to agree with their hateful and angry messages. Television, radio, and the Internet have given them a way to publically condemn other people in God's name. Nothing could be further from the "love your neighbor" message of Jesus.

With so much access to the world news today, we hear of so much evil! Murder, robbery, torture, rape—they seem to be the theme to every news show or Web site.

Have humans become more evil and cruel than ever before, or do we just hear more about the horrors that have been happening?

The last sign of the end that Jesus gives is a happy one! The good news about His message and His plan to save humans will be shared with the whole world! Never before has it been possible to reach so much of the world with good news. Now that the Internet is available on every phone, people can read or hear about Jesus no matter where they live or what language they speak.

How can we be judged worthy by the Creator?

So, is this the time of the end? Can we expect to see Jesus return soon? Yes, we can. But not quite yet.

Three angels shouting

The Bible book of Revelation is filled with prophecies about the future. Many talk specifically about the end of time and the return of Jesus. Chapter 14 tells of three angels flying down from heaven with messages from God (see Revelation 14:6–11).

The first angel is there to share the good news about Jesus to everyone on earth (as Jesus said). He shouts, "Respect God and worship Him. The time has come to judge who has been faithful and who has not." And then, as if there might be some confusion about who he was talking about, he says, "Worship the Creator God, the One who made the heavens and the earth, the sea and the springs of water." It sounds as if the question of creation and where

humans come from is important enough to play a part in how the world ends, or at least a part in deciding who is faithful to follow God and who is not. The Creator is now the Judge.

The second angel shouts that "Babylon is fallen!" Babylon in early Bible history is a place where false religion is born. This seems to refer to the false prophets and religions that are twisting the words of the Bible into lies. As we get close to the end, many religions that claim to be speaking for God will really be leading people away from God.

Then the third angel shouts, "Anyone who worships 'the beast and his image' and gets his 'mark' will feel God's wrath." Other parts of Revelation talk about the beast and his image as powers who try to force everyone to join them in a perverted religion of hate. Those who do join receive the "mark" while those who are faithful to God receive His mark or "seal."

How will we be able to tell which religion is false and which one is following God faithfully? How can we be judged worthy by the Creator? Knowing how God feels

about freedom, we can be sure that the true religion of Jesus will never be about force or hate. It will be people who believe that following Jesus and living as He commanded is the happiest way to live, the best way to live. It will be people who remember the Creator God of Genesis. Could it be that one of the marks of those who are following God faithfully will be remembering the Creation week's celebration of the seventh day?

Everyone will see Him

The time of the end is both the most exciting and the most frightening time to imagine. The day will come when almost all religions go bad—when more and more lies are told in God's name—and true followers will have to fear for their lives. But when that happens, we will know that Jesus' return is almost here.

How will we know when it happens? When Jesus returned to heaven after His time on earth, He rose up into the clouds, leaving His followers staring up after Him. Two angels appeared to them and said, "Why are you standing here staring? Jesus has gone to heaven, and some day, He will return the same way you saw Him go!" (see Acts 1:11).

So we'll be able to see Him coming, in the sky. Other places in the Bible describe Jesus coming in the clouds. In Revelation, it says, "Behold, He is coming with clouds, and every eye will see Him" (Revelation 1:7). So it won't be a secret—everyone will be able to see Him. In fact, Jesus said His return will be like lightning flashing from the east to the west! (See Matthew 24:27.) Jesus even warns us not to believe anyone who says His return has happened in secret.

> The time of the end is both the most exciting and the most frightening time to imagine.

One of the most thrilling descriptions of Jesus' return is in the book of 1 Thessalonians. It says:

> For the Lord Himself will descend from heaven with a shout, with the voice of an archangel, and with the trumpet of God. And the dead in Christ will rise first. Then we who are alive and remain

shall be caught up together with them in the clouds to meet the Lord in the air (1 Thessalonians 4:16, 17).

All those faithful followers of God who died since the days of Adam and Eve will rise up from their graves just like Jesus did. Then they will finally be rid of all the pain and sickness they had in their lives. Now they will be with God forever, along with all the faithful who have lived to see the great rescue.

Conclusion

The rescue operation will be complete when Jesus has returned and put an end to sin and pain and death. When all those who have followed Him faithfully through all the ages of earth are with Him to live as He promised they would.

But the story isn't over yet. We started this journey at the creation of the world. Now we must go there again—for re-creation.

CHAPTER 9

Humans have always lived with the threat of virus epidemics. Spreading by contact, they can move from person to person, infecting more and more people with every hour. You can almost watch it spread through an office of workers or a classroom of children. First one is sick, then another, then another until it seems like everyone is off to see the doctor.

But today, a new kind of virus spreads faster than any before. It can move at blinding speed from one end of the world to the other without so much as a pause for breath. And when it hits, it can bring its target down almost instantly.

Nothing threatens us more often today than a computer virus. In a world where so much of what we do depends on computers, a destructive computer virus can throw the systems we depend on into chaos.

One of the first viruses to spread to other computers by itself was the Melissa virus, unleashed in 1999. Every time it infected a computer, it sent itself out to fifty other computers by e-mail. It spread so fast that even companies like Microsoft and Intel had to temporarily shut down their servers.

In 2000, the ILOVEYOU virus hit computers. It also spread by e-mail, deleting files and opening the infected computers up to an unending flow of junk e-mail. It infected more than fifty million computers in just nine days. Several military sites had to shut down their networks completely until the virus was cleaned up.[1]

> When Jesus came to earth to show what His Father was really like, when He died to pay the price for the human rebellion, the sin virus was defeated.

Though it's not always true with humans who are infected, computers can be completely restored to health. When the virus is gone, everything is just like it was before the infection.

Cleaned and reset

In some ways, that's what happened to the earth. In its original state, creation was beautiful and perfect, with no sickness, no pain, no death. Then it was infected with the sin virus—the rebellion against God. Quickly, the results of that infection spread until plants were rotting, insects were biting, and people were dying.

But the God of Creation is a God of relationships. He created humans with special gifts, gifts that made them like Him. He didn't create unthinking robots—He created free, curious, and clever people to be His companions and friends. When the sin virus spread, His—no, Their (God the Father and Jesus)—five-part plan went into action. When Jesus came to earth to show what His Father was really like, when He died to pay the price for the human rebellion, the sin virus was defeated. When He returns to earth at the end, the sin virus will be wiped clean.

We've imagined the scene when Jesus returns. The sky is lighted with His glorious appearance, as the dead who followed Him rise up to meet Him in the air. And His followers who are alive rise up to join them. That leaves only those who chose to stay in rebellion against God left on earth. That is when God destroys sin. Those who hold on to it are destroyed also.

The Bible talks about a millennium—a thousand years of peace in heaven for the followers of Jesus while Satan is bound to this earth (see Revelation 20:1–6). At the end of this time, Jesus moves His home—His city, the New Jerusalem—to earth, and Satan is destroyed forever.

The New Jerusalem

That is when creation is reset and restored to what it had been in the beginning. In the Bible book of Revelation, the prophet John describes what God showed him:

> Now I saw a new heaven and a new earth, for the first heaven and the first earth had passed away. Also there was no more sea. Then I, John, saw the holy city, New Jerusalem, coming down out of heaven from God, prepared as a bride adorned for her husband (Revelation 21:1, 2).

A new earth! Earth re-created, and this time God will live right there with His people. And none of the evil from the old earth will be there. "And God will wipe away every tear from their eyes; there shall be no more death, nor sorrow, nor crying. There shall be no more pain, for the former things have passed away" (Revelation 21:4).

What is heaven?

Close your eyes. Imagine the most peaceful spot in the world. Is it on a beach, soothed by the endless dance of the waves? Or next to a mountain stream, with a breeze stirring the nearby leaves? Maybe it's in the middle of a snow-filled meadow, with nothing above you but a blazing carpet of stars.

> At the end of this time, Jesus moves His home— His city, the New Jerusalem—to earth, and Satan is destroyed forever.

All of those places sound heavenly. But how long can you rest there? An hour? A day? Maybe a week, with good food and good friends? Maybe longer, but sooner or later, you'll be bored. Humans weren't meant to do nothing for long. We were meant to do things, to go places, to achieve goals.

Many times when people talk about heaven, they talk about sitting on clouds, or playing harps, or singing in choirs. Is that what heaven is like? How does the Bible describe heaven? Writing during a time when the Jewish people had been taken from their homes and forced to live in a distant country, the prophet Isaiah describes this distant future in words that met the longing in their hearts:

They will build houses and dwell in them;
 they will plant vineyards and eat their fruit.
No longer will they build houses and others live in
   them,
 or plant and others eat. . . .
They will not labor in vain,
 nor will they bear children doomed to misfortune;
for they will be a people blessed by the Lord,
 they and their descendants with them (Isaiah
   65:21–23, NIV).

Heaven to them was a home to call their own, the ability to work in their own fields and harvest the fruit of their labor. A place where their children would be safe. Isaiah goes on to describe a place where even the wild animals would not be feared.

> "Then the lame shall leap like a deer."

The wolf and the lamb shall feed together,
The lion shall eat straw like the ox,
And dust shall be the serpent's food.
They shall not hurt nor destroy in all My holy
   mountain . . . (Isaiah 65:25).

A safe place. A place to call home. No worries about thieves or murderers or any dangers. Knowing that your family would always have enough food. How does that sound? But what about being healthy and strong? Isaiah wrote about that as well:

Then the eyes of the blind shall be opened,
And the ears of the deaf shall be unstopped.
Then the lame shall leap like a deer,
And the tongue of the dumb sing (Isaiah 35:5, 6).

Will there be a need for rest in heaven? Perhaps there
will be if we are tilling our own vineyards or harvesting
our own fruit. But whether or not there is a need for rest,
it seems that the seventh day Sabbath rest will still be
available.

"For as the new heavens and the new earth
Which I will make shall remain before Me," says
     the LORD,
"So shall your descendants and your name
     remain. . . .
And from one Sabbath to another,
All flesh shall come to worship before Me," says
     the LORD (Isaiah 66:22, 23).

We will still have a special time set aside to spend on our relationship with God. This reminder of the first creation will be with us forever, it seems.

Heaven for us

What would heaven be to us if we could describe it today? What is the longing of our hearts? Besides of a place of peace and safety, with no injuries, no pain, no sickness, what would we wish for?

> We will still have a special time set aside to spend on our relationship with God.

Think about the wonders of the universe we looked at earlier. What would it be like to visit Betelgeuse in Orion? To study a nebula from close range? To stare into a black hole? What would it be like to travel the universe, seeing things we've only imagined—and things that are still beyond our imagination?

Maybe you've only wished that you had time to learn about astronomy and the stars? Or maybe you've always wondered about geology and rocks? Maybe you've stared at clouds, wanting only to understand how they form into such interesting shapes? Heaven would be a place where you had time to study and learn and explore any subject or object about which you were curious.

> What would it be like to travel the universe, seeing things we've only imagined?

Your interest might first be more personal. How much time would you spend with your loved ones—the ones you lost to death too soon? Now you can be together again. Or those who lived too far away or whom you rarely saw? Now you have all the time in the world!

And take it a step further—what about those relatives that you never met? Your great-grandparents or their great-grandparents? How many questions would you have about their lives and the times in which they lived? You could spend time with every ancestor who was there, all the way back to Adam and Eve!

Maybe you want to learn more about special moments in human history. What would you ask Galileo or one of the first people to have stared up at the stars with the first telescopes? How would they describe how they felt as they began to realize how large the universe must be? What about the first person to see a whale, or a komodo dragon?

Monoceros Nebula

Or maybe you'd have deeper questions. What about the first time Jesus' follower Matthew realized that his Friend and Teacher was really the Son of God? Would you have questions for a person who saw Jesus die on the cross, or saw Him burst out of the grave, alive again?

Would you like to hear the story of how a person like you realized that there really was a God who loved them? Would you have a story to share with others?

Questions for God

Remember the most amazing part of the scene described in Revelation. God brings His city down from heaven to earth—so He can live here with humans forever.

God will be living right down the street from you!

How many questions will you have for Jesus?

What happened with Lucifer? How did he become so angry, so rebellious? Jesus might need to answer those questions through His tears. Perhaps these sad questions can be answered during the thousand years in heaven so that there won't be any tears on the new earth.

Would you ask Jesus to tell you more about creating the earth? Maybe He could explain how He balanced it just right—not too close to the sun, but not too far away. How He gave earth just enough atmosphere to protect life but not so much that it would be too hot. How He used the same DNA pattern over and over for life; how He could make just a little variation in the strands to add up to very different animals.

You'd certainly have questions about His favorite creatures—humans. Did He plan all the variations of skin, hair, and eye color? Did He know how different we could be from each other.

You could ask Jesus about our special gifts! How can we be both logical and creative? How important was it to Jesus that we have free will? Or maybe ask Him, How do we best reflect "Your image"?

His answer to that question might be easy to guess: *"Your ability to love each other."*

And sooner or later we must ask, "Why do You love us so much?"

"Because you are My children. I created you so that I could be with you. And I will do anything so that I can."

Conclusion

The writers of the Bible who tried to describe the last days, heaven, and the new earth sometimes used descriptions that barely make sense to us. They were trying to grasp something that they were only getting a glimpse of, something beyond their ability to understand. They could only express what heaven meant to them, or what it would mean to their people.

We can only imagine those times and those places. Humans have a really hard time grasping the meaning of eternity or life without pain and death. We are limited so much by what we know, by what we have experienced.

But what lies ahead for us in God's heaven is truly beyond imagination. As the Bible book of 1 Corinthians says it:

Eye has not seen, nor ear heard,
Nor have entered into the heart of man
The things which God has prepared for those who
    love Him (1 Corinthians 2:9).

1. http://www.technewsdailycom/2909-10-worst-computer-viruses-history.html.

A New Way
of Thinking

CHAPTER 10

We started this journey with a long look up at the stars. Step outside again, if you can. Look up once more. No matter how many stars you see, you know that there are many more you can't see. Many, many more!

In the same way, perhaps this book has made you think about what else might be out there that you don't see when you look around. The fact that all the stars aren't visible when you look up doesn't mean they aren't there. The fact that God isn't visible when you stare at the sky doesn't mean that He isn't there when you close your eyes and pray.

It's clear that our world is filled with amazing creatures. Their ability to survive and reproduce is so remarkable that it's hard to believe these could evolve accidently. But the abilities of humans are much more impressive. Our free will, our creativity, our problem-solving, our ability to speak and hear—they are unique in this world. These "gifts" have allowed humans to build civilizations, to create art and music, to rocket to the moon!

The Tarantula Nebula

Perhaps the idea that a Creator God gave us these gifts is new to you. It does change the way you see the world. Now you can see that humans should be caring for the

environment. Now you can see that we should be caring for each other.

Having God in our picture of the world explains why bad things happen. We're trapped in a rebellion, a war against God. We have pain and sadness and death. But it also explains that this is not the life we were supposed to have. This is not what God created us to be.

Knowing that God has a plan to rescue us from this rebellion of sin changes the way we think as well. It doesn't stop bad things from happening, but it does help us live with the pain. When we lose a loved one to death, we can hold on to the promise that we will see them again one day in God's heaven.

This new way of thinking does answer the big questions that evolution does not.

- Why are we here? Because God created a unique kind of being—humans.

- Where are we going? In the end, we're going to live with God forever.
- What happens when we die? We wait on the resurrection that is promised.
- Why is there so much suffering in the world? Because we are trapped in a rebellion. But it is coming to an end soon.

Aren't you glad to know that there are answers to our questions, that there is a plan behind the scenes of the world? Aren't you glad to know that the Person who made that plan cares about you?

> When we lose a loved one to death, we can hold on to the promise that we will see them again one day in God's heaven.

"I call you friends"

One of the most amazing things Jesus said is written about in the Bible book of John. On the last night before He was arrested and led to His death, Jesus had a special dinner with His closest followers. He talked to them about His kingdom—about the kind of people He wanted them to be, and the perfect world He wanted them to live in someday.

"I love you," He said to them, "just as the Father loves Me. I have obeyed my Father's commands—followed His plan for Me—so I remain in His love. If you obey My commands—follow the way I have shown you—then you

will remain in My love. I'm telling you this so you can have the joy I have, the greatest possible joy."

And then He repeats something He had said earlier in the evening. In fact, this is something so important to Him that He said it three times that evening:

"This is My commandment, that you love one another as I have loved you" (John 15:12).

You probably hear a lot of Christians talk about what other people are doing wrong. You might hear them talk about how society is wicked and sinful and how everyone needs to change. They might be right—maybe things do need to change. But if they're not talking about caring for the people around them—especially those who need help, then they're not really following Jesus.

Back in our discussion about creation, we talked about how God gave humans special gifts—gifts like free will, and creativity, and the ability to communicate. We said that He did those things because He is a God of relationships. He wanted to have a relationship with the humans He created.

Now we will see what kind of relationship He wanted to have. God wasn't looking for servants who would learn to do as they were told. Or robots who would automatically obey His every command. Listen to what Jesus said to His followers that night:

> Jesus wants His followers to be His friends.

> You are My friends if you do whatever I command you. No longer do I call you servants, for a servant does not know what his master is doing; but I have called you friends, for all things that I heard from My Father I have made known to you (John 15:14, 15).

Friends! Jesus wants His followers to be His friends. He created humans so that He would have more beings who would be happy, curious, thoughtful, loving, friends! He wasn't creating a smarter monkey or an ape that could talk. He was creating something special, something unique in all the universe.

Beyond imagination

Think back to that tour of the universe we took. Can we believe that the same Being who created the 175 billion galaxies in our universe is interested in what happens on this little chunk of rock circling an unimpressive star? If there really are a billion planets in the Milky Way galaxy, what makes this one special?

It would be more than amazing if a Being who could think that big would think of humans at all. It would be astounding that a Creator God with that much power would make a plan to save humans if they rebelled. Now to make it more unimaginable: Not only did God have a plan to save humans—God Himself (Jesus) became a lowly human to do it.

> Jesus wants to teach us, to open our hearts and minds so that in the end, He can call us "friends."

But Jesus didn't come to earth just to straighten out a mess or to teach those misbehaving humans right from wrong again. He didn't come just to find more followers or to make His church of believers bigger than ever.

The God of a universe so vast we can barely begin to comprehend it came to find friends and show them the way back to happiness.

Jesus didn't want creatures who obeyed as instructed. He wanted followers who understood why He came and why living His way was the only truly joyful way to live. Followers who understood those things wouldn't be followers; they would be friends.

That's still what He wants today. He wants to teach us, to open our hearts and minds so that in the end, He can call us "friends."

So how about you? Has this journey given you something new to think about? If a new seed of thought has taken root, open your heart and learn more.

If the universe around us is too big to measure, if the wonders of life are too fantastic to explain, then the love of the Creator God for each one of us is truly beyond imagination.

FREE BIBLE GUIDES

It's easy to learn more about the Bible!

Request: www.biblestudies.com/request

Write: Discover
P.O. Box 2525
Newbury Park, CA 91319

Call: 1-888-456-7933

Study Online: www.bibleschools.com